AEC LORRIES

BILL REID

D1440171

AMBERLEY

First published 2016

Amberley Publishing
The Hill, Stroud
Gloucestershire, GL5 4EP

www.amberley-books.com

Copyright © Bill Reid, 2016

The right of Bill Reid to be identified as the Author
of this work has been asserted in accordance with
the Copyrights, Designs and Patents Act 1988.

ISBN 978 1 4456 6288 6 (print)
ISBN 978 1 4456 6289 3 (ebook)

British Library Cataloguing in Publication Data.
A catalogue record for this book is available from
the British Library.

Typesetting by Amberley Publishing.
Printed in the UK.

Introduction

The Associated Equipment Company (AEC) Ltd was a subsidiary of the London General Omnibus Company (LGOC) Ltd, set up in 1912 to manufacture bus chassis at Walthamstow works in London, with the purpose of supplying the LGOC with buses. AEC was then capable of supplying thirty of the current B-type chassis every week.

After the outbreak of the First World War, AEC production was concentrated on the heavier Y-type chassis for military use. At the end of the war, production dropped and AEC returned to bus-building on behalf of the LGOC. However, there was insufficient demand from the LGOC to support the AEC and other sales avenues, and methods were looked at to keep the company going. Sales to other bus companies were taken up, and lorry production was undertaken alongside the bus chassis.

A move was made to a new factory at Southall in 1926, where production was maintained until the closure of AEC in 1979, which, by then, was part of the British Leyland (BL) group of companies. Along the way, AEC had formed a link with Daimler, and vehicles were produced under the Associated Daimler name. AEC also acquired Maudslay Motors and Crossley Motors, briefly keeping these names alive by badging AEC products as Maudslays and Crossleys. Coach-building companies, such as Park Royal and Charles H. Roe Ltd, also came into the AEC portfolio. Thornycroft of Basingstoke was a late acquisition, but as their road-going vehicles were in direct competition to AEC, that side of the Thornycroft business was closed.

Heavy vehicle production continued after the Second World War, with bus and lorry chassis being updated on a regular basis, making AEC the main rivals to Leyland. In 1962, AEC and Leyland merged, with AEC retaining its own identity, and designs, although policy and decision-making was maintained by Leyland, which later led to a takeover of the British Motor Corporation (BMC). The car-manufacturing side of BMC was struggling for survival, while other BMC types, such as Guy and Daimler, were producing essentially rival models to Leyland and AEC.

The struggling BMC car-manufacturing businesses, and the number of heavy vehicles in competition, brought about various economy measures, and much of the BL empire, as it was now known, was rationalised. This led to the complete closure of AEC in 1979.

I have been a road-transport enthusiast and follower since an early age and became familiar with AEC vehicles in the post-war years. I live in the south-west of Scotland, in an area where heavy vehicles stood out against the lightweights like Ford, Bedford, BMC and many others. AEC buses were also in a minority, although Western SMT use them, but in an area generally outside my remit at the time.

The large, imposing AEC radiator always stuck in my mind as something special compared to the lighter makes, which, by the 1950s, were showing signs of styling and becoming similar. When the new Tin Front cab became available on the 1950s AEC Mercury range, and the other heavy types, I thought these lorries had taken on a tremendous style, but had not lost their AEC identity, by virtue of the new grille being fitted in a modernised version of the old, upright style. I also noticed that AEC double-deck buses fitted with a version of the Tin Front looked a lot better than their contemporaries.

When painted in the traditional Scottish style, with good signwriting and adornments, the AEC lorry looked superb. By the later 1950s, it had become my most-admired type. My late father, who was a lorry driver, always said that he would like to have been given an AEC Mercury or a Leyland Comet to drive. He was to fulfill that ambition in a way, as his last lorry was an Ergomatic cabbed Leyland Super Comet, so he had the best of both worlds.

With the coming of the Ergomatic cab in 1964, which was fitted on Leylands and Albions, AEC lorries lost some of their AEC identity, but still ran with AEC engines and running gear. Some people say that, if BL had developed the AEC side of the company, rather than the ill-fated Leyland 500 series, a much better range would have resulted. That did not happen, and the older AEC designs were discarded and finally put to rest in 1979.

Apart from lorries and buses, AEC provided their range of engines and gearboxes to other UK manufacturers and had links in Scandinavia and Holland with Vanaja and Verheul. The AEC Mercury engine was fitted to a special concrete mixer chassis model of the Albion Reiver for more power output to drive the transit mixer. Guy Motors used the AEC chassis and axles from the Mammoth Major Mk III ranges for its Invincible six- and eight-wheelers and offered the appropriate AEC engines as well.

Throughout the life of AEC, the vehicles, whether lorries or buses, were held in high regard by management, drivers and those maintaining them. It is such a pity that AEC became a casualty of merger and rationalisation. What would a present-day AEC look like had the company survived, and who would be the owners?

This B-type bus is the origin of the AEC. The LGOC developed the bus in 1910 and, in 1912, the AEC was set up to build the vehicles for LGOC and for operators outside London. It had a four-cylinder engine and chain-type gearbox, with worm rear drive. Up to thirty-four passengers could be accommodated. Over 900 of these buses were sent to France during the Great War, as troop transport.

For war transport, the War Department requested a heavier chassis than the B-type, resulting in the Y-type being built as a 3-ton military lorry. After the war, AEC continued to produce the Y-type as a 5-ton lorry.

A Y-type in civilian livery. This one was originally built as a military lorry and was converted to a charabanc in the 1920s. It lay derelict until discovered in the 1960s, after which it was restored as a lorry of the early 1920s.

AEC went through the 1920s, manufacturing various small lorry models in association with Daimler. The vehicles were known as Associated Daimler. The association did not last long, and AEC returned to being a stand-alone company by 1929, when a range of new lorries and buses was produced. One of the new types was known as the Mammoth, which could be built as two-axle, three-axle and four-axle models. The vehicle shown had a gross weight of 19 tons, but was not introduced until 1931. The multi-axle variants were known as Mammoth Majors.

The Majestic was a bonneted version of the two-axle Mammoth and was rated as a 6-tonner. Having the same engine as the Mammoth, it was a useful drawbar unit as shown. A lighter lorry with a four-cylinder engine rated as a 4-tonner was also available. By this time, all AEC lorries and buses were fitted with this tall radiator design, which was to remain in production until the 1950s.

In this picture are a Monarch and a Matador, fitted with early transit cement mixers and driven by their own power units. The Monarch was a lighter alternative to the Mammoth, while the Matador was designed to pull trailers, although it was fitted with a four-cylinder engine.

The Mercury was designed as a lightweight bonneted lorry for loads of 3 tons. The alternative was the Monarch with the same specification, but with forward control and a slightly heavier load rating.

The AEC Mammoth Major 8 was the first eight-wheeler built by the company at the request of a customer. The Mammoth Major 6 was restricted by law to 19 tons gross, and the customer required a lorry with a larger load capability. A second steering axle was fitted to a Mammoth Major 6, allowing it to run at 22 tons gross, thereby increasing its carrying capacity. A large number of Mammoth Major 6 lorries became eight-wheelers, by this conversion. Some Mammoth two-axle lorries were converted to Mammoth Major 6 specification to allow a reasonable load to be carried rather than the 6 tons of which they were capable, in law. The lorry pictured is an early member of the famous Sutton fleet, very much in evidence today.

An early 1930s version of a Monarch with a semi-open cab, which has survived into preservation. Other AEC types around this time were Rangers, with low-height bonneted chassis intended as coaches, but some were used as lorries, especially tankers, because of their low centre of gravity.

The Mammoth Major was a popular choice in the south of England, and Express Dairy operated this one in London and the Home Counties. It survived and has been subjected to an amazing restoration.

Express Dairy used many AEC lorries, and this picture shows a later version for the Mammoth range. It is a lighter weight six-wheeler with what we would call a 'tag axle' today. They were factory built and given the name of Mammoth Minor. They would probably be expected to carry the same loads as their heavier brothers.

In preservation is this fine Mammoth Minor restoration on a bonneted chassis, looking as if it has lost a rear wheel. These lorries were fitted with the wheel dish facing inwards, or had a centre dish wheel. Bonneted and forward control was an option on most AEC lorry models.

The Bracebridge Mental Hospital AEC Monarch has been in preservation for many years. It probably survived through its being a rugged type that did not suffer the hard work normally associated with tippers.

A Mammoth Major 8 Mk II dating from 1935 and another that has made it into preservation. The Mk II eight-wheeler was a lighter version than its predecessor to enable a better payload within the restrictions placed on commercial vehicles by the Road Traffic Act of 1933.

A 1937-registered AEC Matador that appears to have been in fairground service before restoration. It would be an ideal showman's lorry, with its drawbar specification.

An older Mammoth definitely on fairground service. This lorry was registered in 1933, in the early production years of the type, and has survived into the late 1950s or 1960s, if the Leyland lorry in the background, itself a late 1940s registration, is anything to judge by.

Lewis Bros of Minsterley would have taken this Mammoth Major 8 Mk II into their business in 1938. The Mk II was generally to be recognised by having a longer radiator.

Bonneted Matadors were rare, and this artic type may not have been on the specification sheets and could have been converted from a long wheelbase lorry in Australia, where it is in preservation.

A Mammoth Minor Mk II, with single tyres on the trailing axle, photographed when it was so new that registration plates had not been fitted. The rear wheel covers, or 'spats', must have been a pain in the event of a puncture!

S. H. Spratt & Co. have a small fleet of restored AEC lorries, and this Mammoth Major 6 has been beautifully restored as a platform lorry in traditional green and red. The Spratt vehicles can be seen at vintage events in the Midlands.

First registered with Berkshire County Council in 1937, this Matador may not have been originally registered when new, as production of the type ceased in 1935. Again, it has survived into preservation.

Instantly recognisable as a former bus, this is a 1932-registered AEC Regent converted to a fully enclosed lorry to carry emergency equipment for use in various incidents occurring within the London Transport fleet and the Underground.

Bowaters were suppliers of newsprint to the major national newspapers and had a fleet of AEC lorries. Registered in 1935, this Mammoth Major 8 is typical of the fleet, with deep skirts on the platform body.

Registered in the Republic of Ireland, there is no doubt from the marking on the diesel tank that this is a Mammoth Major 6. It is a Mk II and has been fitted with a Duramin cab. AEC did not supply cabs, and dealers would send the chassis to coachbuilders for fitting, which means there was a great variety in cab styles right up to 1964, when the Leyland Group Ergomatic cab was fitted across the AEC range.

At the beginning of the Second World War, AEC production of lorries and buses was turned over to military equipment. During the 1930s, AEC had produced a 4×4 lorry in conjunction with Hardy, a specialist in this field. That work and experience led to the AEC Matador, which was designed as a gun tractor and heavy general service lorry. All branches of the military used them in wartime.

After wartime use, the Matador became surplus to military requirements, and many were sold to civilian service, due to their four-wheel drive capability. Showmen and circus operators were quick to put them into service as generating tractors. The Matadors were fitted with winches, which added to their usefulness.

The Matador was considered an excellent recovery truck by virtue of its winch and four-wheel drive arrangement. Many were purchased by bus companies and put into service as heavy tow trucks. Some were used without modification, while others were fitted with elaborately styled bodies, using bus body components. This Lincolnshire example has been fitted with a coach-style front end.

The East Midland bus company used Leyland National windscreens and front-panel items to produce a more modern-style recovery truck at the front end, but the chariot-style rear end harks back to an earlier era.

Here, we see a Matador in use by a showman at a fairground, presumably generating power for the rides. No evidence of the wartime body can be seen, as it carries the rear-end panels of a Plaxton coach of the late 1950s. The panels have been seriously modified with a radiator grille and lights to suit their travelling in the opposite direction!

A Matador that has had less modification over its life and has survived into preservation. The original-style military cab is retained, with a ventilated roof, which may provide some cooling in high temperatures.

The Western SMT bus company had extensive engineering capability and rebuilt vehicles to their needs. This Matador, one of several, has been extensively rebuilt with a half-cab bus-style body and a Gardner 6LX engine.

A Bedford in a book about AEC lorries! No, this is yet another example of a Matador being modified, in this instance with a Bedford KM cab. The Matador was considered an excellent machine for timber haulage, and this one has a tree-loading crane fitted, seen here in the travelling position.

W. H. Malcolm is the largest haulier in Scotland and, over the years, has had several recovery units. This is a Matador built at the behest of the present CEO and fitted with a Volvo F86 cab. Underneath the cab was a Volvo engine, while other parts were replaced by modern components. Note the air-braking actuators on the rear axle.

Often referred to as a Matador, the 6×6 version was a combination of the Matador front end and military Marshal rear axle equipment. Most were used by the RAF as fuel bowsers with 2,800 gallon tanks. This one has been rebuilt as a timber-haulage tractor and crane, and it survived into preservation. They did not have an AEC name, but were known simply as the 0854 type.

The 0854 type was also used as a tow truck, and the preserved example seen here has been extensively altered by a former AEC dealer. Apart from the complete replacement of the military body and cab, normal road wheels have been fitted. Oswald Tillotson was a prominent AEC dealer and cab builder until the mid-1960s.

The wheel turns full circle. A Matador, which was purchased after military service and converted by a Scottish bus company to a tow truck, is now returned to wartime condition by a military vehicle enthusiast.

Not a Matador, as such. The Douglas Equipment company converted Matadors as a commercial enterprise, mostly as timber tractors and winch vehicles. In this instance, an AEC Mk III-style cab has been fitted with a Douglas radiator.

In the immediate post-war years, the UK government was pushing the manufacturing industries to export as much of their output as possible. As a consequence, new lorries were in short supply and alternative measures were taken. This picture shows a very large pantechnicon van on an AEC chassis, which was the basis of a double-deck London AEC Regent bus. Other makes of wartime utility bus chassis were used in this way for high-capacity haulage.

A Bonallack-bodied AEC Mammoth Major eight-wheeler being loaded aboard a ship, in pursuance of the government edict of exportation. There is a possibility that it carries an ACLO rather than an AEC badge, which was a marketing name for AEC in some South American countries. The upper section of the cab will be stored within the body.

The Bonallack cab was a rarity in the UK, and this could be the only one in preservation. It is a neat style, doing away with the prominent radiator, and it has bus-style, deeply angled windscreens, said to reduce glare, in keeping with the emphasis on export.

As a means of modernising an apparently old-style truck, this Mammoth Major 6 has been fitted with a large cab, somewhat reminiscent of Thornycroft cabs of the 1950s. The cab envelopes the normal AEC radiator and appears wider than usual, perhaps to accommodate three crew members, which was often the case in the drinks-distribution trade. Windows in the cab roof are an unusual feature.

Blue Circle had a large number of short wheelbase tippers, and AEC lorries were not strangers in the fleet. This AEC Mammoth Major is typical of 1950s eight-wheel tippers with only enough space between the axles for a fuel tank, or a spare wheel. It was new in 1948 and would have been rated at 22 tons gross vehicle weight (GVW).

AEC produced a four-wheel lorry for the UK market, along the lines of the Mammoths, but with a smaller engine, and rated at 12 tons GVW; it carried the Monarch name. This one has been in preservation for many years, in the East of England Transport Museum, near Lowestoft.

An AEC Mammoth Major Mk III that was part of the Rowlands Amusements fleet, seen here on a very quiet dual carriageway. It carries a modernised cab with wrap-around windscreens on the old-style, exposed radiator scuttle and may well have been part of the Wincanton Transport fleet, which was a large user of AEC lorries.

Another AEC Monarch in preservation and taking part in the Trans-Pennine Road Run some years ago. Preserved in the name of a Manchester haulier, it was probably used in the textile trade where AEC lorries were popular.

An AEC in fairground use. It appears to be a Monarch and may have been specified as a drawbar unit. It certainly has been used by the showman with trailers, as a substantial front towing bar has been fitted for close trailer manoeuvring.

This is a post-war former military fuel bowser, on a Mammoth Major 6 chassis, generally associated with the Royal Navy. It was sold off by the military; the refuelling equipment was removed and then had a platform body fitted, for use as a preserved lorry.

The heavy articulated lorry was second to the eight-wheelers in the early 1950s, although every premium manufacturer had a model available. AEC applied the name Matador to their post-war artic units. This one was new to Devon County Council for low loader and tipper duties.

In the early post-war years, AEC began taking over commercial vehicle manufacturers, with Maudslay Motors, of Alcester, being one. Maudslay built lorries and buses in a range competing with AEC, using AEC engines in some models. Maudslay remained on the market for a few years, but had become AEC models bearing the Maudslay name. This is a so-called badge-engineered AEC lorry marketed as a Maudslay Mustang, beautifully restored by John Thomas.

The AEC Mammoth Major Mk III is well represented by this eight-wheeler taking part in an Ayrshire Road Run and seen in Portpatrick harbour, warming up for the journey ahead. This one is a former fuel tanker and has been in preservation for a long time.

An AEC Mammoth Major Mk III with the short wheelbase tipper chassis. It was on display at a CVRTC Classic Commercial Motor Show, at Crick, in the 1990s. Note the traditional wooden body.

Another AEC Mammoth Major Mk III kicking up dust as it enters the site of an AEC rally in recent years. This one is fitted with the Duramin cab, recognisable by its recessed door handles and swaged panels. The faired-in headlamps are an unusual feature.

This Matador, in preservation, was being used as a drawbar tractor for a large fairground organ. The chassis appears to have been extended, as the Matador artic unit would not have been as long as this.

British Road Services (BRS) was a large buyer of AEC lorries when it began replacing older lorries that were taken into possession on nationalisation. The AEC Mammoth Major was the predominant AEC type, and this well-used example is typical of BRS lorries in later life.

During the 1950s, the heavy artic tractor became known as the Mandator. Also during that time, the heavy chassis could be specified with a version of a cab fitted to the new range of AEC Mercury lorries. Again, the cabs were not fitted by AEC, except for the scuttle panel, allowing variations in design. It was known as the 'Tin Front' cab.

A Tin Front cab on a Mammoth Major in fairground use. It is seen here as a six-wheeler lorry, but may have been an eight-wheeler in a previous use. The showmen are well known for removing the second steer axles.

Another Tin Front Mammoth Major wearing a cab very similar to that shown on a Lucozade lorry earlier in the book, but with the new style radiator grille then to be found on AEC lorries and buses alike.

This battered, but recently painted, Mammoth Major on the fairgrounds carries a Scottish registration and may be a former BRS lorry. The operator is part of the Scottish Codona fairs family.

AEC was associated with fire appliances over most of its history. In the post-war years, the AEC Regent bus chassis was used by many fire brigades as a basis for appliances. The bus chassis, suitably shortened, made a robust platform for pump escapes, such as this one, which ran from South Shields fire station.

The 1950s were the era of the AEC Militant, classified as a military 10-tonner. These were massively engineered lorries, built as 6x4 and 6x6, with a heavy trailer towing capacity. They lasted with the military until the introduction of Scammells and Fodens.

The AEC Militant was much larger than the older Matadors and saw less civilian use after being 'demobbed'. The majority in civilian use became heavy recovery trucks, like this one, and were fitted with a variety of recovery equipment.

The Militant, like the Matador, was favoured by bus companies as a heavy recovery truck. This one has been completely transformed from its military appearance by clever use of bus body parts and windscreens.

Western SMT also thought that the Militant chassis would be a good base for a heavy recovery truck, and this is their modification, using some of the original cab parts. This particular vehicle was restored and rallied for a number of years and is still extant, but somewhat neglected.

The military specified some AEC Militants as complete recovery trucks. Former recovery operator Seaplane Motors is seen here with their later version, with a Tin Front style cab, recovering an accident-damaged bus.

Alan Syme, of Newtyle, near Dundee, is an AEC enthusiast, and his recovery fleet contained many much-modified examples. His Militant looks fairly standard, except for extra front ballast. *Tayside Retriever* is a very appropriate name for a recovery truck.

Because of their inherently strong build, Aberdeen County Council had a number of Militants for use as snowploughs. This one still has its military body, which would have carried ballast weights.

Some Militants went into fairground use, and this one with John Harris Amusements was probably used as a tractor, pulling trailers on the road, and as a recovery truck on soft ground. The finish of the vehicle is immaculate, as seen on all Harris vehicles.

Another immaculately finished Militant in basically unaltered condition. This was operated by William Rowe & Sons Ltd. It is still a long climb up to the cab even with the non-military step added.

Some 4x4 versions of the Militant were made, but were perhaps too heavy for the role and few were produced.

Coles Cranes fitted their products to AEC Militant chassis, making a lightweight crane for military use, which were subsequently taken into use by civilian users. Note the yellow Coles triangle in place of the familiar AEC blue triangle.

Another Coles Crane on a Militant chassis, this time beautifully restored. Compared to today's cranes, the safety equipment on the jib appears rather rudimentary. This one also carries the yellow Coles triangle badge.

Like the older Matadors, the Militant has had its modifications. This one has been fitted, rather neatly, with an Ergomatic cab normally fitted to road-going AEC lorries. The driving position in the cab looks normal, so presumably other control modifications have taken place below the cab.

The AEC Mammoth Major moved into the Mk III type in the 1950s, which were well favoured by the fuel companies. By the time this one was new, the GVW for eight-wheelers would have been increased to 24 tons, allowing extra payload for not much more unladen weight. This example has had an excellent restoration, reminding us of the various liveries used by petrol companies before private haulage contractors took over fuel distribution.

BRS continued to buy AEC products through the 1950s, and when there was a move towards more articulation, the AEC Mandator was a proven type at 24 tons GVW. This one is carrying an early type of demountable load carrier referred to as a 'Lancashire Flat', a precursor to today's universal ISO containers.

Glasgow Corporation Transport were still buying AEC Matadors in the 1950s, and this one was later rebuilt from standard, using the upper-deck windscreens and roof dome of the then Walter Alexander bus bodywork. This one survived to take part in an event at the Scottish Bus Museum when it was located at Whitburn, before Lathalmond, in Fife.

Another survivor in restoration is an AEC Depot Matador with a hefty set of recovery equipment. The yellow-and-blue livery appeared on all AEC-owned vehicles.

By the mid-1950s, AEC had designed and started production of a lighter lorry that was to compete with the Leyland Comet models. Initially, it was designed for 12 tons GVW and was heavier than the Leyland Comet but, when 14 tons GVW was allowed in 1955, the Mercury had a distinct advantage. The Mercury introduced the Tin Front style cab that could be specified on the Mammoth Major types. Roger Flavell is seen arriving for an Ayrshire Road Run in his Mercury.

Shell Mex and BP used a lot of AEC chassis as the basis of fuel tankers. Here is a medium wheelbase Mercury, restored in exactly the way these lorries are remembered in their working time.

The Glasgow showman G. G. Hanley had this Mercury, a former fish lorry from Aberdeen, rebuilt as a van and made capable of pulling trailers. While the Mercury was a powerful lorry on its own, it was not intended as a drawbar outfit. Husband and wife Brian and Helen McGinley restored the Mercury quite a number of years ago, and it can be found touring the rally scene every summer.

The registration PVC 885 was issued to this AEC Mercury in late 1954, which means it is a 12-tonner. The handsome coach-built body has the early style Mercury radiator grille with two extra vertical strips that were soon removed.

The Mercury was built by AEC in the traditional way and left the factory as a chassis and scuttle, going to a preferred coachbuilder to be fitted with cabs. As before, this resulted in slightly different cab styles. By the late 1950s, the style still had separate windscreens fitted in rubber seals and had a more upright appearance, as shown in this Irish platform truck.

On the introduction of the Mercury range, some fire brigades opted for this model, which was lighter than the Regent bus chassis. Edinburgh Corporation Fire Brigade, later Lothians & Borders Fire Brigade, had a turntable escape ladder fitted on to this long wheelbase Mercury, which was retained in use for a long time.

Of the various cab styles fitted to the Mercury, this pair – thought to be on their delivery run, unpainted, to the erstwhile Oswald Transport, of Ayr – has cabs built by Boalloy, incorporating the new style AEC grille. These cabs were also fitted to heavy Guy lorries, which, incidentally, used AEC chassis and other components.

The AEC Mercury was made available in different wheelbases, which included an articulated tractor version. This one, in service with a Northern Ireland milling company, would have had a nominal gross combination weight (GCW) of 18 tons, but it is coupled to a four-in-line trailer, which was considered a two-axle trailer, and in the pre-plating days of the 1950s and 1960s, lightweight artics often ran at the maximum GCW of 24 tons, or more. The Mercury would be struggling at that weight, but many were used at that GCW.

BRS was a large customer for AEC Mercury artic units when it began to change to articulation, and many were bought as nominal 10-tonners. This one, registered in 1962, has the later style cab, which seems taller, and narrow in depth. It is running on smaller tyres, indicating it is intended as a medium load carrier.

The Newton fairground family maintained their lorries in a very good outward condition, and their AEC Mercury was no exception. They also had a much older ERF 5.4G in the same condition.

Easily recognised as a former fire appliance, this Mercury has performed as a vintage tractor transporter for many years and is a show vehicle in its own right. With the fire brigade, it carried a turntable fire escape. Note the heavily plated chassis behind the crew cab.

The AEC Mercury range had a short wheelbase option for tippers, and this late model, from 1965, shows such a lorry that has survived well enough to enter preservation. This photograph shows it prior to its restoration. This model was phased out in the mid-1960s, in favour of the new tilt cab design, which was also seen on Leylands and Albions.

Smith, of Maddiston, was a well-known large fleet, with subsidiary companies around the country. Light and heavyweight AEC artic units were used, and this Mercury coupled to a four-in-line trailer would be expected to carry loads well above its rating. The limit with such a trailer was 24 tons GCW, 6 tons above the maximum for the Mercury, and it would often be running at that gross weight.

Anybody visiting the island of Malta realises that the transport there, including cars, takes them a step back in time. Used British vehicles were to be seen everywhere, and AEC lorries were a well-favoured import. Shown here is a typical Maltese lorry, much modified, but the AEC Mercury cab is still evident. As Malta transport enthusiasts know, it might not have an AEC engine.

The Mercury, in long wheelbase form, made a good showman's lorry. This example was on a fairground in the town of Ayr, possibly thirty years ago. It was new in 1962.

When farm-milk-collection contractors changed to bulk tanker operation, the AEC Mercury with a medium wheelbase was found by many to be a very suitable chassis. David Tod's Mercury, new in 1963, is seen here parked at an Edinburgh creamery, alongside a Tennant Albion, which was also well favoured for this work. Tennant of Forth is still operating in milk collection and general haulage.

An AEC Mercury taking part in a vintage rally in Aberdeenshire, a good few years ago. It had been parked up after use by J. W. Henderson, now Keyline, and was then in need of exterior restoration. Mechanically, it was sounding good. Its present condition is not known.

The London Brick Company (LBC) Ltd was a big user of AEC lorries from early production times. This is evidenced by the number of LBC lorries in preservation. This one was still in use when photographed well into the 1970s, if the Volvo F86 behind it is anything to go by. It appears to have been fitted with a Duramin cab, and although registered in 1962, it has the first style of radiator grille used in 1955. RTS of Hackney also fitted cabs for LBC, some of which had rearward opening doors, known as suicide doors.

Returning to Malta, this rather forlorn-looking AEC Mercury has had some rough painting to the grille. Other than that, it looks a typical Maltese tipper of the 1970s and has been relegated to water-carrier status with a square tank in the tipper body.

An AEC Mercury, bearing a 1965 registration, built as a fire brigade hydraulic escape. It is fitted with an almost standard cab and has sucker-mounted windscreen de-misters, suggesting that a heater wasn't fitted. By 1965, this AEC Mercury was old-fashioned, as the new tilting Ergomatic cab, which came fitted with heaters, had been introduced.

As the AEC Mercury had proved to be a very good four-wheel lorry, some fleet operators upgraded them by fitting third axles, and thereby raising the GVW to around 18 tons. AEC took the hint and began to manufacture a six-wheeled Mercury and named it Marshal. Like the Mercury, it became a popular lorry because of its light weight, which allowed an almost matching payload to the traditional heavy six-wheelers.

Jas. McKinnon Jnr was an Ayrshire haulage contractor and bus operator who had a liking for the AEC marque as lorries and buses. This was one of his bulk-feed tippers that put in a lot of off-road work going to farms. It is a late model, from 1965, soon before the change to the tilt cab models.

In the course of time, the AEC Marshal found its way into fairground use as it had a long chassis, ideal for carrying the multitude of showman's paraphernalia. Again, this is a late model, from 1965, and is fitted with a single-piece windscreen, modernising the look of the cab.

AEC built a further three-axle version of the Mercury, and it was known by the old Maudslay name of Mustang. The twin-steer Mustang (or four-in-hand – a horseman's term used in some areas) was usually built with a short rear overhang to equalise the axle loading. This is Richard Cresswell's beautifully restored and maintained Mustang attending a truck show in the Midlands.

The twin-steer lorry fell out of favour after two-axle lorries were uprated to 16 tons GVW. Heavy twin-steer lorries had a GVW of 17 or 18 tons and had no great advantage over the modern two-axle lorry. This Mustang has been converted to a recovery truck, to prolong its use.

AEC had a range of heavily built off-road tippers, which were referred to as Dumptrucks. They began with the purpose-built Mammoth Major Mk III, with reinforced chassis, leading up to the Mk V, which found popularity with heavy civil engineering companies. The bonneted type shown here had a 10 cubic yard capacity. Some of them lasted in service for many years. Manufacturing of this type passed on to Aveling-Barford, another British Leyland (BL) company, and subsequently to Scammell, where it was known as the LD 55. An artic unit version was known as the Bush Tractor.

An AEC Dumptruck, when new, with a very large, but light-looking dumper body, possibly for the movement of coal.

AEC introduced a new range of Mammoth Major and Mandator heavy chassis in 1959. This range replaced the Mk III models (there was no Mk IV range) with a much more modern appearance. The front axles were set back, allowing for a cab to be fitted with a step before the front wheel, giving better access and egress. The cab had a resemblance in style to the later Mercury models, but still was not built by AEC. Various cab builders used slightly differing designs, with Park Royal's (an AEC company) being the prominent type.

The new style made for a handsome lorry, although the rather upright cab did not provide a lot of internal space, considering a large engine cover dominates the interior. The restored example shown here is very typical of a long-distance lorry of the early 1960s.

The AEC Mandator Mk V looked very similar to the eight-wheelers from the front, but was built on a very short wheelbase, as was the general practice of the time to allow for a semi-trailer of 24–26 feet in length.

Bath & Portland Stone were regular users of AEC Mammoth Majors, going back to
the original Mammoths. This good restoration project has depicted a 1960s Bath &
Portland Stone lorry, but carries an Essex registration number, issued in 1963, so may
not be original.

The Mandator Mk V was in the vanguard of articulation, when many hauliers were
turning from rigid eight-wheelers to the advantages of semi-trailer versatility. This
1965 Mandator is a late model and is shown coupled to a four-in-line trailer, which
was considered suitable for 24 tons GVW. This type of trailer was a little lighter than
a tandem axle, and tyre scrub was eliminated.

Febry's Transport, from Gloucestershire, were long-term AEC users, as well as most other British makes, in the 1950s and 1960s. Their Mammoth Major Mk V Fleet No. 128 looks in good condition, while waiting to set off with a well-roped and sheeted load.

A number of heavy-haulage tractor units were built as Mammoth Majors, and this Mk V initially served with the Royal Navy as a ballasted tractor. It has been restored, depicting a civilian heavy-haulage tractor of the early 1960s.

A dealer publicity photograph of a Mammoth Major Mk V when new and about to enter service in County Fermanagh, Northern Ireland. The typical short wheelbase of the time is highlighted, with just enough space for the spare wheel on the chassis.

In later life, the Mammoth Major Mk V became well used on the fairground circuit. Many of these AEC lorries were cast off by hauliers turning to articulation and were ideal load carriers for showmen.

The new Mammoth Major cab was fitted to the forward-control Mk V Dumptruck. These lorries were built long after the new Ergomatic cabs were introduced in 1964 and were to be seen on construction sites for many years.

The late John Ward, of Oadby, rebuilt and restored this Mammoth Major Mk V to his standard, which was that of a working lorry, from a chassis/cab, which had been shortened for use as a recovery truck. After being worked hard in that role, it had been left to the elements and was in a sorry condition.

Claben Transport was a large Scottish fish haulier, for their own products, and other fish dealers. Their livery was well known around the country wherever the UK fishing fleet was landing fish. The very slim front-to-back length of the cab is highlighted here.

Bassett's Roadways is a large fleet still operating in Staffordshire. Before the coming of the European makes, Bassetts used most of the UK heavyweight lorries available. This AEC Mammoth Major Mk V has been set aside in the Bassett yard, after a long, working life. It looked like a fairly easy restoration, at the time of the photograph.

Two more Mammoth Major Mk V chassis being used by showmen, in this case, the erstwhile Billy Smart's Circus. Both appear in good condition, although rust has taken hold on the door of the one on the left. The cabs have been built by different coachbuilders. A close look shows differences around the doors.

The Mandator Mk V was also available as a long two-axle type. Very few were used on haulage, probably because of their weight, and most were found in military use as refuellers, some with low profile tanks and a very basic cab, to allow air transportability. A version was specially built to RAF specification, as a transporter for Blue Steel missiles, and it had a half cab and bus-like bonnet.

The Mandator Mk V served for a long time with the armed forces, and this one was 'demobbed' and registered for the road in 1966. It has a rather unconventional cab, with sliding doors, that looks as if it were designed by a committee!

Taking the Mk V cabs into consideration, this one looks very smooth and tidy. Again, it is slightly different with flat windscreens. This is a Mammoth Major 6, rebuilt as a recovery truck; it may have been in use as a military ballasted tractor.

The W. H. Malcolm fleet did not contain many AEC types. This one, said to be an original in the fleet, was acquired for the Donald Malcolm Heritage fleet and is seen here taking part in a Scottish Road Run, being driven by Bob Tuck, the well-known transport writer.

Another variation of the Mandator cab of the early 1960s, restored as a Christian Salvesen lorry of that period. This cab uses flat screens too, but has a more rudimentary square-backed design, full of windows.

The Mid-Ulster AEC Group restored this fine Mammoth Major Mk V as a timber transporter. It was fitted out with sleeping accommodation among the load of logs, which accounts for the sheet over the front log stow, on the very wet day of the photograph.

AEC, as already said, had a good export market, and many orders came from the Benelux countries in Europe. The trucks were supplied, as in the UK, as chassis/scuttle, or chassis only. This Belgian Mandator has a locally built cab, very much in the style of European coachbuilders. It is possibly a Mandator from the later tilt cab range, distinguished by its low build.

While the Mk V range of lorries were being produced, AEC was busily exporting around the world. At the time, there was a demand for bonneted lorries, and AEC was able to supply them. The bonneted export models had the marketing name of Mogul and were supplied to many developing countries. The alternative name of ACLO was used by AEC for South American orders.

Not all of the bonneted Moguls went abroad, and some were used where overall length restrictions were less of a problem. This Mogul served with the London haulier Annis & Co. Ltd, which was well known for its use of 'interesting lorries'. Two are depicted here, looking not unlike the purpose-built Scammell and trailer combinations.

Seen at a Great Dorset Steam Fair is a fine-looking Mogul with an extended cab. It is carrying an Aveling-Barford built version of the bonneted Dumptruck.

In 1964, the UK Construction and Use Regulations were changed to allow higher maximum gross weights on heavy lorries. A 16-ton GVW was permitted on two-axle lorries, and AEC were soon to produce a new style of Mercury for that weight. It had a radically different cab, known as the Ergomatic, which tilted and could also be fitted to Leylands and Albions. The cab had a lower driving position and was said to be logically, and ergonomically, laid out to suit all drivers. Unfortunately, the lowered cab came with an engine cover that sloped upwards from the windscreen. The Mercury seen here was turned out in a true Scottish livery of red and black, with gold signwriting.

This photograph of an AEC Mercury chassis and cab shows the chassis frame was straight and almost free of clutter. The fuel tank was fitted on the nearside. This lorry had been set aside for preservation in the 1990s, but whether restoration work was carried out is unknown.

The new Mercury range was available in different wheelbases, from artic unit to tippers, to haulage types. To allow a GVW of 16 tons, the tipper wheelbase became, by necessity, longer, and this insulated tipper is typical. This particular Mercury was the last in use in the county of Ayrshire.

Traditionally, the AEC marque was always favoured by fire brigades, and this long wheelbase chassis formed the basis for a turntable escape ladder with Dorset Fire Brigade. The low-mounted Ergomatic cab was well-suited in this application, where the ladder extended over it.

This is a later model AEC Mercury with a simplified grille. Earlier cabs had grille patterns that suited the three different name badges (AEC, Leyland and Albion). Early cabs also had the mirror arms fitted to the doors between the quarter light and the main window, but they were susceptible to road dirt, and were later positioned on the windscreen uprights, being viewed through the windscreen.

A short recovery truck based on a Mercury artic chassis. The grille panels are different on this cab and were to be the last change before production ceased.

A late model Mercury with an R plate, and the radiator grille panel more often seen on Leyland Lynx and Buffalo lorries. It may have been fitted to replace the rusted or damaged original panel. It carries a domestic fuel delivery tank and appears to be near the end of its operational time.

This is a fine example of a restored AEC Mercury. Four-wheel, 16-ton tippers always had a place in tipper haulage until a change in the rules allowed six- and eight-wheel tippers an upgrade in their gross weights. By the 1970s, heavy four-wheel tippers began to fade away in favour of six- and eight-wheelers, which could carry more and had better operating margins.

The AEC Mercury was well favoured as a long, bulk-haulage tipper. There was a simplicity to the chassis, and the cab allowed easy access for a driver who might be in and out several times in a day. This example looks well used, but has been well looked after by the driver, evident from the lack of dents and scrapes.

Usually, an AEC Mercury fitted with hydraulic aerial equipment would be a fire appliance. Good use has been made of the long wheelbase chassis and the low cab to allow fitting of the hydraulic hoist, which appears to have a considerable reach.

An AEC Mercury with a crew cab outside the fire brigade was unusual. This one, photographed in fairground use at the Beamish Museum, in County Durham, was originally used by a safe manufacturing and fitting company, hence the need for the crew cab. To that end, it has a hydraulic lift on the rear, which would have been a boon to the showman owner.

The long wheelbase AEC Mercury was always a firm favourite as a livestock transporter. The longest wheelbase allowed cattle containers up to 26 feet in length, and many were fitted out with a third collapsible deck for sheep transport. Some were used with trailers, but would be somewhat underpowered.

Peter Bannister in his beautifully restored Mercury bulk-feed tipper, which he had previously used in his business. The larger engine fitted to the Mercury produced more power over contemporary 16-ton tippers and would have been an advantage on farm deliveries.

The new Mercury range had an artic unit rated for 24 tons initially and subsequently at 26 tons in 1970. This made it a useful middleweight artic unit, and many were used with tandem axle trailers and were almost indistinguishable from the heavier Mandators. The engine tone was the giveaway. There is no type badging on this example, so it could be a Mercury.

As with the previous AEC Mercury range, there was a six-wheel version for 22 tons GVW. The existing Mercury engine was used, and it coped well enough with the higher weight. Again, it was named Marshal and could be had with 6x2 or 6x4 drive. Short and long wheelbase variants were listed, giving a versatile range. London Brick had a large fleet of Marshals, alongside their Mercury fleet; this one being a tipper on a medium wheelbase.

An AEC publicity photograph showing a brand new Marshal about to be delivered to its first owner. It is not an early model, as it has the BL logo badge in place of an AEC triangle. It is from the time when super single rear tyres were thought to be an advantage in tipper work. Note the small Dennis lorry under cover.

In the early 1970s, the well-known Reid's Transport fleet was being built up, and new lorries were being acquired. Three AEC Marshals are seen lined up in the then Ayr yard. These lorries were medium wheelbased tippers and operated on long-distance grain haulage.

David Ritchie, from Carrbridge, in the Scottish Highlands, runs a fleet of tippers and skip loaders. Included in the fleet was this AEC Marshal, in all its working glory, taking part in a small truck show.

The Marshal was favoured by livestock transporters and, with its higher GVW, was better suited to carrying livestock in three decks, although this one is not fitted with a third deck. It has been well used and shows evidence of rust on the front panel. This type of cab was always susceptible to rust, and good cabs or panels are in high demand by restorers.

One of the largest haulage fleets in Wales is that of Mansell Davies & Son. It is predominantly a Volvo fleet in the present day, but all marques have been used over the years. Shown here is an AEC Marshal alongside two of its fleet brethren. The lorry in the centre is a Leyland Lynx, carrying the same cab, but with a different front panel, sometimes found on AEC cabs.

As a long wheelbase platform lorry, the Marshal suited a lot of needs. The Kent Turf Company had a long-bodied lorry, which would have worked well for them with palleted turf being easily loaded, and at 22 or 24 tons GVW, capable of carrying a decent load.

Colas Roads had a need for good-capacity tar tankers, and the AEC Marshal provided a very suitable chassis for their tar sprayers. This example had seen a lot of use when photographed and had been set aside to provide parts for the considerable numbers of AEC lorries in the fleet.

In 1971, the GVW of a six-wheeler was uprated to 24 tons, and some AEC users thought the Marshal to be just a little underpowered at that weight and suggested that a larger engine should be fitted. The outcome was the Marshal Major that was fitted with a downrated Mammoth Major engine, giving a good increase in power and torque.

Conoco Fuels were another user of the Marshal Major in the 1970s. This one, seen in a yard beside an early Seddon-Atkinson, has an untidy cloth or paper radiator muff.

There is no type name on this well-looked-after recovery truck in the fleet of London-based Len Vasler. It could be a Marshal, but it would be better suited to its role, if it had the Marshal Major specification.

A Marshal Major, which made it into preservation, was this long wheelbase platform lorry, in the name of Tillside Haulage, being one of the three preserved AEC classic show lorries belonging to this owner. The Marshal Major could take about 15 tons of load, being heavier than the Marshal, which could manage 16 tons with a light body.

Another restored Marshal Major is a heavy bus-recovery unit from the old Nottinghamshire Barton's fleet. It is carrying a rather old-fashioned lifting jib, which may have been manually operated. It is difficult to say if it is a former tipper chassis, or has been shortened to suit recovery work.

Export models of AEC six-wheelers tended to have heavier chassis, such as this Mammoth Major being used in New Zealand. With its three-axle trailer, the AEC looks a real heavyweight, but it needed six axles to run at a decent gross weight. Axle-weight restrictions are quite low in New Zealand, compared with Europe.

The next step up in the weight range was to eight-wheelers and Mammoth Majors. There was a 24-ton GVW Marshal eight-wheeler, but it was only marketed for a year. The Mammoth Major in various wheelbases was rated over the years between 26 tons and 32 tons, as six-wheelers and eight-wheelers. This rather tired example was on internal duties at ECC Quarries and was carrying a large tank, possibly for water, inside the tipper bodywork. Note the route of the exhaust pipe to prevent dust being stirred up.

Old AEC lorries were well liked in Malta, and many were exported to that country. Much modification took place in Malta, and this Mammoth Major looks as if it has been shortened, which is still a common Maltese engineering practice on tippers.

Another Maltese AEC, which may be a Mammoth Major, or it might be a Marshal with an added steering axle. Such are the wonders of the Maltese modification art that a Marshal was fitted with the cab from a Dodge Commando. That must have taken a lot of work.

Cyprus is another Mediterranean island that imports used UK lorries. This AEC Mammoth Major had recently arrived from the UK and had just been painted before use. The UK registration plate may or may not be removed!

Hopefully not doing any more recovery work, this Mammoth Major picture is inserted to show how rust takes hold in the Ergomatic cab. Whether it could be saved or be scrapped is open to discussion!

This well-used AEC Mammoth Major could be at the end of its working life with Clyde Cement. A trade plate is displayed, and it may be heading for disposal. Speculation suggests that the bulk cement tank will be refurbished, for use on another chassis, and the Mammoth Major could find its way to the fairground circuit.

Here is a Mammoth Major on the 'fairs'. It is an early version, registered in 1966, and has been fitted with an open-top showman's body. The lorry looks in good order, but may have had a cab replacement, hence the Mandator badging on the lower panel.

Eight-wheel timber, or logging, lorries were good for stability, but they declined after the introduction of 44-ton artics, or lorry and trailer combinations. Some soldiered on, and this Mammoth Major was still hauling timber in the first few years of the New Millennium in the Malvern Hills area.

The new Mandator for 32 tons came into production with the Ergomatic cab, as fitted across the then AEC range of lorries. Initially, most Mandators were used at 30 tons GCW with tandem axle trailers to comply with axle loading and length restrictions. A combination of five axles were required to run at 32 tons GCW. This superbly restored Mandator worked for E. & N. Ritchie among many other AEC types.

Road Services (Caledonian) Ltd was formed when parts of the nationalised BRS were sold off. The 'Caley' developed into a large Scottish fleet, and this Mandator, new in 1967, is coupled to a tri-axle tanker trailer to allow 32 tons GCW running.

The AEC Ergomatic cab was designed for drivers who did not, as a rule, sleep in their cabs. The cab depth was only 48 inches from front to back, and with a large engine cover intruding, space was at a premium. Moreover, the engine cover was offset to the left to give the driver more space, making the passenger-side space quite restrictive. In later years, when drivers' hours rules were changed, AEC never produced a sleeper cab, but conversions were made, as seen on this example. It must have been a rudimentary sleeping area.

The AEC Mandator in the late 1960s was probably the highest-powered, standard British-made artic unit. Spiers of Melksham ran a large fleet of them, many being used units refurbished before use. As can be seen in this photograph, the Mandator was a compact unit, and the height of the engine cover is clearly visible. This high engine cover was standard across the BL range of lorries using it, even when a small engine was fitted.

R. & W. Febry used a number of Mandator artic units, and this 1968 model, seen here coupled to an acid tanker, shows off the grille panel and the AEC names badges as they were in the early years. Note the lack of safety features on the sulphuric acid tanker, compared to modern times.

A fairly nondescript Mandator, in traditional livery, with a Crane Freuhauf trailer marked for TIR work. For a few years, the Mandator, like the Leyland Beaver of the same era, could be specified with a semi-automatic gearbox. This one has a rudimentary sleeper box added to the cab.

A fine AEC Mandator that has been in preservation for a long time. It was a Spiers of Melksham working lorry and had been restored in Spiers livery. It later passed to Scotlee Transport, of Irvine, Ayrshire, where it was refurbished and painted in the Scotlee colours.

Again, a standard Mandator unit. It does not have the AEC triangular badge, which has been replaced by the BL, the so-called Catherine Wheel corporate logo. When this lorry was new, it could run at 32 tons GCW on four axles.

In 1968, AEC introduced a V8 engine for the Mandator, with a power rating of 250 bhp. This was a powerful engine by British standards of the time, but it was not successful. Only a handful of V8 Mandators went to British operators compared with thousands of the six-cylinder type.

The V8 engine was small enough to be accommodated below seat level, eliminating the high engine cover, and two passenger seats could be fitted.

The Mandator was also marketed as a long wheelbase drawbar unit. Few entered service in the UK. This one from southern Ireland, with traditional Irish livestock bodies, has been restored and can be seen at Irish vintage events.

Looking like a Mercury, this Maltese tipper is more likely to be a Mandator artic unit. With the larger Mandator engine, the lorry would be more suited to the rigours of Maltese overloading than a Mercury. That was the theory, at least, but it could be confounded by local engineering!

From 1964 to 1970, UK artics required five axles to run at 32 tons GCW. Some three-axle trailers were built, but their excessive tyre wear through scrubbing did not endear them to haulage men. AEC designed the Mammoth Minor artic unit, which was essentially a Mandator, with an extra steering axle and a longer wheelbase. It was designed to use tandem axle semi-trailers and comply with axle-weight regulations, without the excessive tyre wear of a tri-axle trailer. This photograph at a former haulage yard in Carlisle shows the layout of the Mammoth Minor.

This Mammoth Minor artic unit survived into preservation and can be seen at vintage events around the country. It is pictured attending a CVRTC show with a modern tri-axle trailer, which is a bit anomalous, as the unit was designed to eliminate the 1960s version.

Over the years, AEC bus and coach chassis were used as the basis of high-capacity vans, with old double-deck bus chassis becoming large pantechnicons. In this instance, an AEC Reliance PSV chassis has been used to produce a long, low van, where space to carry boxes had priority over weight. Clarkes Boxes used other PSV chassis, such as the then Bedford VAL, to create large vans.

This photograph shows another AEC Reliance chassis, which had been fitted with a Spanish Salvador Caetano coach body, typical of the 1970s. It was later converted to a horse box with somewhat angular accommodation for the horses. With two or three horses aboard, the steering must have been interesting!

Another AEC Reliance coach chassis that has been converted to a recovery truck by the Walsh Brothers, of Liverpool, by way of removing the rear of the Plaxton Panorama body and fitting a crane and a load bed. The vehicle being carried looks like an Albion, and the brothers probably restored it in a very short time, which they are renowned for.

Being heavyweight trucks, AECs were prime targets for conversion with recovery gear. This one is either a Mammoth Minor twin-steer unit or a Mammoth Major eight-wheeler, with its trailing axle removed.

As seen in the section about AEC Militants, Alan Syme at Newtyle Commercials was a great fan of AEC. He has carried out various modifications on this one, which is probably a Marshal Major, for greater power. A sleeper cab has been fitted, of more generous proportions than previously seen, as he used his machines on very long-distance recovery.

What may be referred to as a 'Showman's Special', the cab badging refers to this as being a Marshal Major, meaning a six-wheel lorry, with an axle removed. Or, is it simply a long wheelbase Mercury with a refitted grille panel?

G. H. Lucking run a large fleet of vans on theatrical removals, around the UK and Europe. The work would have entailed a busy schedule, not taking into account breakdowns, or worse. Their recovery unit was a Mammoth Minor, from the wheelbase length, and would be powerful enough to cope with large pantechnicon vans. Did they make a song and a dance about it? Probably not.

A heavyweight recovery unit from Portugal with a locally built cab in the flamboyant style of the time. The low-set driving position suggests that it is built on a Mammoth Major chassis, which would normally have been fitted with an Ergomatic cab.

Today, we have the so-called crossover cars. Could this AEC Regent come into that category as a crossover from a bus to a lorry? A tidy job, cutting it down from a double-deck bus to a tow wagon with space on the rear to carry equipment.

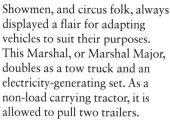

Showmen, and circus folk, always displayed a flair for adapting vehicles to suit their purposes. This Marshal, or Marshal Major, doubles as a tow truck and an electricity-generating set. As a non-load carrying tractor, it is allowed to pull two trailers.

In the 1930s, AEC produced three 8x8 load-carrying tractors, which were capable of pulling two, or more, trailers. One of these, known as a Colonial Tractor, worked in the Australian Outback for many years and was the basis of the Australian road trains seen today. It has been restored and is in the Transport Hall of Fame at Alice Springs. Two AEC enthusiasts decided to pay homage to the Colonial Tractor and built a close replica from two AEC Matadors with 8x8 drive and steering on the outer axles, as in the original. It is entitled Mammoth Mongrel!

The Leyland Marathon, which was to be Leyland's answer to Volvo, Scania and the other Continental types, which were making their presence felt in the UK market in the 1970s. It was built at the AEC factory, in Southall, and was seen by many as the successor to the Mammoth Major and Mandator ranges. It did not enjoy the success and enthusiasm previously known at AEC. This was the last new design to come out of Southall before AEC production ended.